AF316637

How to Be Chill

365 Ways to Find Peace in a Noisy World

How to Be Chill

365 Ways to Find Peace in a Noisy World

Phillip Bankss

weldonowen

BREATHE DEEPLY

When you feel overwhelmed, pause and take a deep breath to reset your mind and body. This can help calm your nervous system.

EMBRACE SILENCE

Silence is a rare and precious gift in a noisy world. Embracing quiet moments helps you reconnect with yourself and find clarity in your thoughts.

TRY SAYING WHAT YOU'RE GRATEFUL FOR ALOUD TO YOURSELF

Gratitude opens the door to contentment and calm. It reminds you of the good things in life, no matter how small.

WAKE UP TO WATCH THE SUNRISE

Nature's daily light show is a reminder to slow down. Take a moment to soak in the colors and appreciate the beauty. It's a peaceful way to start your day.

PRACTICE POSITIVE SELF-TALK

Be kind to yourself, especially on tough days. Talk to yourself like you would a good friend.

ENJOY A FAVORITE SNACK

Treat yourself to a snack you love, and eat it slowly, savoring every bite.

VISIT A LOCAL COFFEE SHOP

Something about a neighborhood coffee shop helps bring a wave of calm and perspective. Working or enjoying a slow cup of joe surrounded by community is very *chill*.

DO ABSOLUTELY NOTHING FOR FIVE MINUTES

Give yourself permission to just be. Sit quietly, close your eyes, and let your mind wander.

PRACTICE SAYING NO

You don't have to agree to everything. Saying no can be a small and powerful act of self-care.

MEDITATE DAILY

Even a few minutes of meditation can work wonders. It can help you let go of racing thoughts and find a peaceful center. Make it a daily habit for a calmer mind.

JOURNAL YOUR THOUGHTS

Writing things down helps clear your mind and process emotions. Don't worry about grammar—just let your thoughts flow. Journaling can be a private escape to peace.

FOCUS ON ONE THING AT A TIME

Multitasking can make you feel scattered. Slow down and give your full attention to one task. You'll feel more in control and less stressed.

ENJOY YOUR FAVORITE MEAL

Notice the flavors, textures, and aromas of your favorite food. Mindful eating turns meals into moments of calm.

REREAD A FAVORITE BOOK

Get lost in a story you love. Reading can transport you to another world and give your mind a break from stress.

FIND A SPOT TO SIT IN THE SUNLIGHT

A little sunshine can lift your mood and help you feel more at ease. Find a sunny spot and soak in some vitamin D. Don't forget your sunscreen—getting a sunburn is not so chill!

DECLUTTER YOUR SPACE

A tidy environment can help soothe your mind and make the small tasks in life feel more manageable. Take a few minutes to clear off a surface or organize a drawer.

UNPLUG FROM TECHNOLOGY

Set aside a block of time each day to disconnect from screens and reconnect with yourself. You'll be surprised how much more regulated you feel without constant stimulation.

DRINK WATER SLOWLY

Hydrate with intention. Water works wonders for our health. Savor each sip and notice how it refreshes you.

LISTEN TO A CALMING PODCAST

Find a podcast that soothes your mind, whether it's about mindfulness, nature, or stories.

WATCH THE CLOUDS

Lie back and watch the clouds drift by. Let your thoughts float along with them or see what shapes you can carve out.

LAUGH OFTEN

Laughter is nature's stress reliever. We can often get tense and take things too seriously. Just let yourself be silly and find laughter wherever you can.

LISTEN TO GENTLE RAIN SOUNDS

Even on sunny days, gentle rain sounds can be incredibly soothing. Play them in the background to create a peaceful atmosphere while you work.

LIGHT A SCENTED CANDLE

A gentle fragrance can transform your mood and environment. Choose calming scents like lavender, sandalwood, and patchouli to help you unwind and relax. Let the soft glow and aroma invite calming energy into your space.

TAKE A POWER NAP

A short nap can recharge your body and mind so you wake up feeling refreshed. Thirty minutes or less is an ideal amount of time to help you avoid grogginess for the rest of your day.

MAKE A VISION BOARD

Cut out images and words that inspire you to create your very own vision board. Visualizing your dreams can be calming and motivating at the same time.

TRY ESSENTIAL OILS

Essential oils like bergamot or chamomile can help you relax. Diffuse them in your space or dab a drop on your wrist.

TRY WOOD WHITTLING

Carving a figure of your choice out of a chunk of wood is not only a great talent to develop, but it is also unique and relaxing.

COMPLETE A CROSSWORD PUZZLE

Allow your mind to focus on something like random words and clues for a nice break from responsibilities and brain fatigue.

BEDAZZLE YOUR FAVORITE BOOK

Bedazzling hardcover books is a fun trend that can bring some of your favorite titles to life with 3D jewels and bright colors. Place your bedazzled book on display in your home.

KEEP A FIDGET HANDY

Fidgets are perfect for moments when you can't quite keep still and chill. Keep a fidget or two handy in your car or bag for when you need something to do with your hands.

PICK UP A YO-YO

The slow up-and-down movement of a yo-yo makes this a simple and relaxing toy that keeps its charm no matter your age.

TRY SKETCHING WITH CHARCOAL

Charcoal is a deep and buildable medium to work with in art. Try sketching with charcoal and learning to emphasize smudging, shading, and contrast.

SET BOUNDARIES

Protect your time and energy by setting healthy boundaries. You'll have more space for what truly matters when you are not compromising your comfort for other people or tasks.

WATCH A NATURE DOCUMENTARY

Let stunning visuals and soothing narration transport you to a calmer place while learning about the nature around you.

GIVE YOURSELF A GENTLE HAND MASSAGE

Rub your hands with lotion and gently massage your fingers and palms. It's a small act of self-care that feels surprisingly good.

TRY MINDFUL YOGA

Yoga doesn't have to be intense. Try gentle poses and slow movements that can help you unwind.

MAKE A CUP OF HOT COCOA

This sweet drink warms the body and tastes delicious. It may even offer you a bit of nostalgia, which brings on the chill. Don't forget to top it with mini marshmallows.

WRITE A LETTER TO A FRIEND

Writing a letter and connecting with someone you care about can lift your spirits. Handwritten messages also hold a special sentiment in this technology-focused world.

PRACTICE FORGIVENESS

Forgiveness—for yourself and others—frees you from carrying heavy emotional baggage and crowding important areas of your life and mind.

MAP!

JOIN A TOUR OF YOUR CITY

If you ever feel stagnant where you live, try going on a guided tour of your city. Learning new and exciting details about the place you call home can bring a fresh perspective and sense of appreciation.

BAKE SOMETHING SIMPLE AND SWEET

The act of baking, with its comforting smells and hands-on steps, is pure chill. Focus on the process, not perfection.

LIGHT INCENSE

A favorite incense stick can set a peaceful mood. Let the scent fill your space and your senses.

ENJOY A WARM BATH
Soaking in warm water relaxes your muscles and calms your mind. Try adding Epsom salts or essential oils for extra-chill vibes.
FLEA SHAMPOO

TRY COLORING WITH ALCOHOL MARKERS

The practice of coloring is pretty chill in itself, but using alcohol markers that blend and shade so seamlessly is especially satisfying.

SPEND TIME WITH ANIMALS

Animals have a way of making everything better. Cuddle or play with a pet, or just watch videos of animals in their habitat to feel more relaxed.

PLAY A GAME OF SOLITAIRE

Enjoy some time to yourself with a calming game of solitaire, a relaxing way to pass the time while exercising your mind.

WRITE DOWN A GRATITUDE LIST

Write down three things you're grateful for every day. It's a simple practice that shifts your focus to the positive.

REMIND YOURSELF TO LET GO

Release what you can't control. Ruminating on something you can't change is anxiety-producing, and letting go is a solid path to peace.

MAKE YOUR BED EACH MORNING

A tidy bed can make your whole room feel calmer and start your day off right. It's a small act with a big impact.

LOUNGE IN COMFORTABLE CLOTHES

Ditch the tight, restrictive stuff and slip into something cozy. Comfort helps your body relax, which makes it easier for your mind to follow.

SPEND TIME SOLO GARDENING

Getting your hands in the dirt is grounding—literally. Helping something grow in the earth connects you to nature and gives you a sense of accomplishment. Even a small windowsill garden can bring a bit of peace and clarity.

WATCH THE STARS

Head outside on a clear night and gaze up. The vastness of the universe puts your worries into perspective. Let yourself feel small and awed.

TRY GENTLE TAI CHI

Tai Chi is like meditation in motion. The slow, flowing movements help release tension and bring you into the present moment.

LISTEN TO WIND CHIMES

The soft, random sounds of wind chimes can be surprisingly calming. Hang some near a window and let the breeze do the rest. Be mindful of your neighbors to keep this extra chill.

TAKE A WALK IN NATURE

Nature's beauty and tranquility help reduce anxiety and promote relaxation. A simple walk can be a powerful act of self-care and a chill way to move your body.

VISIT AN AQUARIUM TO WATCH FISH SWIM

Aquariums are mesmerizing. Watching a fish glide through a large body of water is calming and visually pleasing.

PLAN YOUR IDEAL STRESS-FREE VACATION

Think of where you would have the most stress-free and relaxing vacation, then start planning your trip there. Even if it is a bucket-list destination, start manifesting!

RECORD A VIDEO DIARY

Try recording a video diary daily, weekly, or monthly. These videos feel like venting sessions that can leave you feeling lighter and at ease. They can also be fun to watch back over time.

VISIT AN ART MUSEUM

Take in the art and scenery of your local museum. Appreciating different artists from your community or art from all over the world can help you feel inspired and creative.

TAKE A BREAK FROM THE NEWS

Getting caught in the constant news cycle can be overwhelming. Give yourself permission to take a break from all the headlines occasionally.

EAT A SNOW CONE OR ICE-CREAM CONE

Enjoy a snow or ice-cream cone from a local shop. Savor the chill treat and think of fun flavors to try.

DO A FIVE-MINUTE STANDING STRETCH

Standing up for a gentle stretch helps you release tension and feel more at ease. Just move in ways that feel good to you—your body and mind will thank you.

WATCH A COMEDY SHOW OR STAND-UP ROUTINE

Put on your favorite comedy or stand-up special and let yourself laugh out loud. Humor helps you see life's lighter side.

USE A WEIGHTED BLANKET

Weighted blankets can help reduce anxiety and promote relaxation. Snuggle under one for instant calm and a hug simulation.

PRACTICE BODY SCANNING

Close your eyes and mentally check in with each part of your body. Notice any tension and breathe into those spots. This practice grounds you and helps release stress.

DO A PUZZLE

Focusing on a puzzle distracts your mind from stress and gives you a sense of accomplishment as you watch it form into something before your eyes.

MAKE A "CHILL CORNER" AT HOME

Designate a spot in your home with cozy pillows, a soft throw, and maybe a plant or two. Retreat there whenever you need a break.

MAKE A LIST OF POSITIVE ACTIONS YOU'RE PROUD OF

Big or small, our actions make an impact, and reminding yourself of your power to move positively in today's world can inspire confidence and calm.

GO FOR A RELAXING BIKE RIDE

No need to race—just cruise. Feel the wind on your face and notice your surroundings. Let each pedal stroke melt away stress.

WATCH A CLASSIC MOVIE

Old movies have a nostalgic, comforting feel. Pick a favorite classic and let yourself be transported to another time.

DO A RANDOM ACT OF KINDNESS

Helping others boosts your own mood. Hold the door, pay a compliment, or send a kind message—good vibes multiply and help spread the chill.

MAKE SIMPLE ORIGAMI

Folding paper into unique shapes is calming and creative. Follow a video tutorial and enjoy the process, not just the result.

BURN YOUR WORRIES

Write your worries down on paper, then burn them in a fiery release. Just seeing all your big worries written down and dwindling into ash can help you realize they're not so big at all. Remember to do this in a controlled, fire-safe environment, like a firepit outside.

GAZE AT THE MOON

The moon's calm presence is a reminder of the universe's rhythms. Take a few minutes to look up and feel connected to something bigger.

LISTEN TO A FAVORITE ALBUM FROM START TO FINISH

Albums tell a story—let yourself get lost in the music. No skipping, no distractions—just listening.

CUDDLE UP WITH A BLANKET

Wrap yourself in a soft, warm blanket. It's simple and a nice way to settle into a moment—instant comfort.

LISTEN TO OCEAN WAVES

Ocean sounds are nature's lullaby. Find a recording or video and let the rhythm of the waves wash over you.

TRY A NEW RECIPE

Cooking something new can be a fun, mindful activity. Focus on each step and enjoy the process and your delicious result.

SIP HERBAL TEA

A warm cup of herbal tea is like a hug as it washes over you from the inside. Chamomile, peppermint, and lavender teas are especially soothing. Take a moment to savor each sip, and let your worries melt away.

TRY A GENTLE FACE MASSAGE

Use clean fingertips to massage your temples, forehead, and jaw gently. This can release tension and help you feel more at ease.

VISUALIZE A PEACEFUL PLACE

Close your eyes and imagine a calm, beautiful spot. Visit it in your mind whenever you need to relax.

TRY BIRD-WATCHING

Bird-watching is peaceful and requires patience. Even just watching birds from your window can help you feel more present and relaxed.

TRY FOREST BATHING

Spend time in a forest or park, simply being among the trees. Nature's energy is grounding and restorative.

PRACTICE BOX BREATHING

Inhale for four counts, hold for four, exhale for four, hold for four. Repeat. This simple breathing technique is a fast track to calm.

REMEMBER TO BE OKAY WITH BEING MISUNDERSTOOD

While being heard and understood is important, you won't always be understood by everyone. Remember to know who you are and focus on the people in your life who do help you feel understood.

· JUST A CHILL GUY ·

PAINT A SELF-PORTRAIT

Get creative in how you see yourself. Painting can be wonderfully meditative and helps you tap into your creativity. Don't worry about the result—just enjoy the process.

TRY LEARNING TO PLAY AN INSTRUMENT

Take on the challenge of learning a new instrument. This can help you test and strengthen your patience and commitment to learning.

LISTEN TO CALMING SOUND FREQUENCIES

Put on a playlist of sounds from the solfeggio scale. These can help calm anxiety and reduce stress just through mindfully listening.

SIT IN A SAUNA OR STEAM ROOM

If you have access, let the heat relax your muscles and clear your mind. Breathe deeply and enjoy the warmth. Let your worries drift away with the steam.

SQUEEZE A STRESS BALL

Stress balls are a silly and simple way to release a bit of stress and frustration. They're easy to take with you, so you can squeeze one if you encounter a high-stress situation on the go.

SLOW DOWN ON DAILY TASKS

Take your time completing your daily tasks and enjoy finding beauty in the mundane moments.

DON'T TAKE THINGS TOO PERSONALLY

Always make sure you are being treated with respect, but also remember that sometimes people just don't mean to offend. Know the difference between disrespect and miscommunication.

HANG OUT WITH THE WINDOWS OPEN

Enjoy a fresh breeze moving through your home. Relaxing with the windows open can help air circulate through your house and reduce the chances of harmful air being trapped inside.

WATCH A RELAXING MOVIE

Watch a movie with no loud explosions or fast car chases. Try something slow and satisfying to help calm and entertain you.

GET A FULL-BODY MASSAGE

If you can, try visiting your local spa for a full-body massage. This is a wonderfully calming experience that helps your body feel relaxed and realigned.

DOODLE FOR A WHILE

Let your pen wander on the page. Doodling is a simple, creative way to relax your mind.

WATCH A TIME-LAPSE OF FLOWERS BLOOMING

Nature's slow magic is mesmerizing. Watching flowers bloom reminds you that beauty unfolds in its own time. Let yourself be patient and present.

LISTEN TO SOFT INSTRUMENTAL MUSIC

Instrumental music creates a soothing backdrop for any activity and has been proven to help with focusing. Let the melodies calm your thoughts.

MAKE HOMEMADE POPSICLES

These are a refreshing and easy treat to make at home. You can also be mindful and practice patience while you wait for the sweet treats to freeze.

GO FOR A WALK AROUND YOUR NEIGHBORHOOD

Walking around your neighborhood, even for just fifteen minutes, can help you feel connected to your community and energized from moving your body.

HAVE A GAME NIGHT AT HOME

A good old-fashioned game night is a chill way to have some fun with your friends or family. Make it interesting by choosing a theme, like a whodunit.

SIT IN A HAMMOCK

If you have one, take a few minutes to sway gently. Hammocks are the ultimate chill-out spot.

DANCE BREAK

Stand up wherever you are and bust a move for a minimum of thirty seconds. Being free and dancing is liberating and can help you not feel stuck in a space or routine.

WRITE A SHORT STORY OR POEM

Let words flow without worrying about rhyme or reason. Creative writing is a great way to process feelings and find peace.

WATCH A CHILDHOOD FAVORITE CARTOON SHOW OR MOVIE

Sometimes watching a show or movie from childhood can provide a sense of nostalgia and calm. Think of how you've changed since then.

SING A SONG TO YOURSELF

A low hum or full-out performance of your favorite song can loosen you up and maybe even offer a laugh.

READ A CLASSIC NOVEL, ONE OF THE GREATS

Try reading a book that is considered a classic by the masses. Take some time to chill and see what all the fuss is about.

TREAT YOURSELF TO A NEW ITEM OF CLOTHING OR AN ACCESSORY

If you can, treating yourself to a new item of clothing or a cool accessory can give a little spark to your confidence. Snap a selfie with your new digs and just look at how chill you are.

PRACTICE MINDFUL LISTENING

When someone speaks, really listen. Give them your full attention without planning your reply. It's a gift to them and a practice in presence for you.

PLANT A TREE

Planting seeds and watching them grow into a mighty tree is a peaceful and environmentally friendly way to stay chill.

"I can help others feel chill and heard by listening fully and not interrupting."

TAKE A SCENIC DRIVE

Hit the road with no agenda—just enjoy the scenery. Rolling through new places at your own pace is a great way to unwind.

PB
CHILL

DRINK A GLASS OF REFRESHING CITRUS WATER

A glass of cool lemon, lime, or grapefruit water is refreshing and cleansing. Take slow sips and enjoy the zing.

WATCH AUTUMN LEAVES SWAYING IN THE WIND

Nature's gentle movements are hypnotic. Find a tree, or a video of one, and watch the leaves dance. Allow your mind to drift, and remember to move with the breeze, not against it.

WATCH SOOTHING ASMR VIDEOS

Soft sounds and whispers can be surprisingly relaxing. Find an ASMR creator you like and let their gentle tones soothe you.

MAKE A LIST OF YOUR FAVORITE MEMORIES

Thinking about your favorite memories can help you feel grateful for the life you've lived up to this point. Reflect and be thankful for the good times that are gone and the good times to come.

THINK BEFORE YOU SPEAK

Taking a moment to think before you speak can make a world of difference. This will help you mean what you say to others and avoid moments of miscommunication.

MAKE A CALM-DOWN BOX

Fill a box with things that help you relax—like a favorite book, stress ball, or cozy socks. Pull it out whenever you need a chill boost.

TRY A GENTLE FOOT SOAK

Warm water, Epsom salts, and maybe a few drops of essential oil—soak your feet and feel tension melt away. It's an easy way to pamper yourself.

MAKE A HOMEMADE WARM COMPRESS

There are many ways to make a soothing warm compress at home. Find a tutorial on the internet to begin enjoying a satisfying, heated sensation.

TRY TO NAME THE NATURE SOUNDS YOU HEAR

Whether spending time in a park or just sitting on your front porch, balcony, or stoop, pause to listen to the sounds of nature around you. This is a calming practice that helps bring you back to the present moment if your mind is feeling a bit busy.

ASSUME GOOD INTENTIONS

Give someone a fighting chance and assume they are in your life with good intentions. This helps you relax and not operate from a guarded state.

REMEMBER YOU ARE ONLY ONE PERSON

You are a super human but not *superhuman*. Don't overwhelm yourself with responsibilities or commitments. Take deep breaths and do the best you can.

EXPECT POSITIVE OUTCOMES IN YOUR LIFE

Expecting the best for your life is not always a setup for a letdown. When you envision the best possibilities for yourself, you welcome positive thinking and energy.

TAKE CARE OF A HOUSEPLANT

Houseplants can teach you how to care for something outside of yourself. They add a bit of color and nature to your home and also help purify your air.

PLAN A LUNCH DATE IN THE PARK

Enjoy a nice lunch date in the park. Pick up your favorite bite to eat and lay down a blanket to enjoy a meal on the grass.

HAVE A SLOW SATURDAY

Celebrate making it through your week with a slow-paced Saturday full of relaxation or chill tasks that bring you joy.

GO SWING ON A SWING SET

Remind yourself of the euphoria a simple swing can bring. Throw your head back and swing as high as you can.

HOST A STRESS-FREE GATHERING

Have a few of your favorite people over for a stress-free gathering. Tell everyone to bring a bite or drink to share, dress casually, and enjoy some quality time with your people.

LOOK THROUGH OLD FAMILY PHOTOS

Pictures really do say a thousand words. Try traveling along your family's story through photos.

MAKE A LIST OF ALL THE PLACES YOU WANT TO VISIT

Let your imagination wander. Dreaming of new places can lift your spirits and inspire hope. No passport required.

THINK ABOUT THE JOY OF CHANGE

Life's many changes, whether personal or professional, can easily feel overwhelming. Pausing to see the joy in change helps with adjusting, acceptance, and being present for the new parts of your life.

LISTEN TO AN AUDIOBOOK

Choose a soothing voice and an uplifting story. Let the words take you on a journey as you relax or do chores.

REMEMBER TO WALK AWAY FROM YOUR WORK DESK

Walking away from your work desk to have a decent lunch or to take five minutes for yourself can aid in your productivity and give you a moment to breathe through the shuffle.

FLOAT IN A POOL OR LAKE

If you can, lie back and float on water. The weightlessness is deeply calming. Let your worries drift away with the ripples.

EMBRACE BOREDOM

If you're used to a busy schedule, embrace the feeling of boredom when you can. We don't always have to be on the go.

ACCEPT COMPLIMENTS WHEN THEY ARE GIVEN

Believe the nice things people have to say about you. It's hard to accept compliments when you're not used to them, and even sometimes when you are.

AVOID DOOMSCROLLING

The world can get *bleak* quickly if you spend excessive time doomscrolling or taking in information faster than you can process it. Know when it's time to stop scrolling and go touch grass.

ENJOY YOUR SOLITUDE

There is power in being alone and not lonely. Learn to enjoy your own company.

ADOPT A DAILY MANTRA

Saying an uplifting mantra to yourself daily can help you tackle any challenges that lie ahead. Make your mantra as silly or as philosophical as you like.

LISTEN TO A CALMING PIANO PERFORMANCE

The gentle notes of a piano have a specific calming feeling associated with them. Turn on a video of a pianist playing or listen to a few tracks that heavily feature this classic instrument.

GET COMFORTABLE ASKING FOR HELP WHEN YOU NEED IT

Whatever the scenario, asking for help when you need it is key to self-awareness and not overwhelming yourself with too much at once.

PLAY A VIRTUAL GAME WITH FRIENDS

Try playing a virtual game with friends to help feel connected when far apart. Relax and kick some virtual butt, with love.

WATCH A VIDEO OF SUNBEAMS THROUGH CLOUDS

An image of sunbeams shining through a cloudy sky can be peaceful and symbolic, as it reminds us that there is always something beautiful behind the clouds.

MAKE A GIFT LIST FOR THOSE YOU LOVE

Writing a gift list for loved ones is a great task to focus on if things start to feel not so chill. This also prepares you to combat any gift-giving stress, as you now have a list to reference for upcoming holidays or birthdays.

SPEND SOME TIME IN CHILD'S POSE

A child's pose is an easy way to center yourself and focus only on your body and your breathing. It mimics a feeling of safety and comfort.

PLAY A RAIN STICK

The soft cascade of a rain stick mimics the soothing sound of falling rain. Close your eyes and let the rhythm calm your mind.

GO ON A SOLO DATE TO A NEW RESTAURANT OR BAR

Spend some time trying a new spot by yourself. Dining out alone helps build confidence and appreciation for your power to hold space and have fun on your own.

PHONE A FRIEND TO CATCH UP

The lost art of mindlessly fiddling and talking on the phone for an hour is a great way to stay connected with your friends while navigating busy schedules and adulthood.

DECENTER THE OPINIONS OF OTHERS IN YOUR LIFE

Try not to live your life operating strictly off the opinions of others. It's hard to feel comfortable in knowing who you are or what you want if you only consider the desires and opinions of others.

REMEMBER REST IS ESSENTIAL TO PRODUCTIVITY

No matter how much we try, we simply can't run on empty. Remember to rest so you can show up for yourself and do your best.

DON'T ARGUE WITH STRANGERS (OR ANYONE) ONLINE

It's easy to get swept up in bickering online about issues you are passionate about, but the truth is, the opinions of strangers on the internet don't matter—don't let pride steal your peace.

MAKE A LIST OF THINGS THAT YOU CAN CONTROL

When life feels overwhelming, focus on what's within your power. Let go of the rest. This brings clarity and peace.

DO A GENTLE SHOULDER ROLL

Roll your shoulders forward and back to release tension. It's a nice way to reset your posture and your mood. Even a few seconds can make you feel lighter.

ADMIT TO YOUR OWN IMPERFECTIONS

Striving to be perfect, or to be perceived as such, is exhausting. Remembering that you are an imperfect human can help remove unnecessary pressures and stress.

MAKE A NEW FRIEND

The older we get, the harder making friends can feel. Open yourself to meeting new people and forming meaningful friendships.

PLAN THE LIFE YOU WANT

Remember, you can plan the life you want and go live it!

LEARN HOW TO CROCHET OR KNIT

Knitting and crocheting are treasured, relaxing pastimes. Try your hand at knitting or crocheting by finding a book or video tutorials to help you along.

ORGANIZE YOUR CLOSET

When life gets hectic, small, high-use spaces like closets can easily be overrun with clothing and shoes. Take a moment to organize your closet so getting ready for your day doesn't start with stress.

NAME FIVE THINGS YOU LOVE ABOUT YOURSELF

Reminding yourself of what you love can also remind you of what you can offer to the world. You can name these five things aloud, think of them to yourself, or write them down.

TRY A GROUP WORKOUT CLASS

Motivation can often come from watching others working toward the same goal. Attending a group fitness class can improve your health over time and help you feel connected to others.

PLAY A GAME OUTSIDE

Playing outside is a great way to connect with your inner child and spend time outdoors. Think of how you or your friends used to spend time outside and make an adult version.

WATCH A VIDEO OF WATER LILIES FLOATING

Water lilies floating gently along a stream of calming water is a relaxing visual that can transport you to a moment of tranquility.

SIT BACK AND RELAX IN A ROCKING CHAIR

The gentle motion of rocking is naturally calming. Let yourself sway and relax and enjoy the setting around you.

PRACTICE PATIENCE WITH YOURSELF AND OTHERS

When you are patient with yourself, you're not only helping your own nervous system, but you're also teaching yourself to be more patient with others. A little patience goes a long way.

CELEBRATE YOUR INDIVIDUALITY; DON'T COMPARE YOURSELF TO OTHERS

Comparison is not only the thief of joy but also the thief of uniqueness. Let yourself exist as you are, without comparing your personality or life to others.

AVOID DRAMA AND GOSSIP

Usually, drama and gossip do not add anything meaningful to life; they're more of a distraction from focusing your energy on more important and positive things.

ACCEPT WHEN A RELATIONSHIP IS OVER

Accepting that a relationship with someone you love has ended is often difficult, but that pain will fade, and acceptance can help you move forward and remain present for what's ahead.

KEEP A DREAM JOURNAL NEAR YOUR BEDSIDE

The memory and details of dreams can often escape us. Scribble down your dreams in a dream journal when you first wake up, and take time to look through it occasionally.

TRY NOT TO OVERTHINK SMALL DECISIONS

Allow yourself to be swift and sure in those small life decisions that tend to hold a bit of stress. Like what's for dinner, or the next picture in your Instagram dump.

START A SCRAPBOOK

Scrapbooking is a wonderful way to cherish your memories. Design your scrapbooks however you like and fill up as many as you want to create a personal archive of your life.

PARTICIPANT

"MY NEW CHARACTER"

TRY A MINDFUL SKIN-CARE ROUTINE

Washing your face slowly with products that feel good to you is a great way to stay chill. You'll feel the benefits of a mindful skin-care routine immediately and see the long-lasting results over time.

TRY A NEW SPORT OR PHYSICAL ACTIVITY

Hike! Give a new sport or exercise a try. Moving your body increases your happiness and helps you feel accomplished and in tune with your health.

LEARN HOW TO WRAP A PRESENT PERFECTLY

A nicely wrapped present and the act of wrapping one is oddly satisfying. Practice perfecting your corners and spiraling your bows for the next gift you give.

MAKE A PITCHER OF DELICIOUS, ICE-COLD LEMONADE OR TEA

A nice, cold pitcher of fresh lemonade or tea is a quick beverage to make and offers a sweet reward. Try enjoying a chill glass on a warm day.

MAKE SHAVING CREAM ART

The texture of shaving cream is a sensory dream. Mess around in the soft foam and make a masterpiece of your own.

PRACTICE TRUSTING YOURSELF

Second-guessing yourself on every decision can lead to a lot of anxiety and unhelpful hesitation in life. Practice trusting yourself and having confidence in your inner voice.

REVAMP AN OLD ITEM OF CLOTHING

Remind yourself that you *do* have something to wear already in the closet; maybe it just needs a little love. Try revamping old items of clothing with subtle or major alterations to give them new life.

GO READ A BOOK IN THE PARK

Diving into a good book is relaxing on its own, but doing so in a calm park with good weather adds a whole new layer of chill.

TRY BUILDING A BIRDHOUSE

Make a home for the flying fowl friends that visit your yard. Building something with your own hands offers a sense of accomplishment and joy.

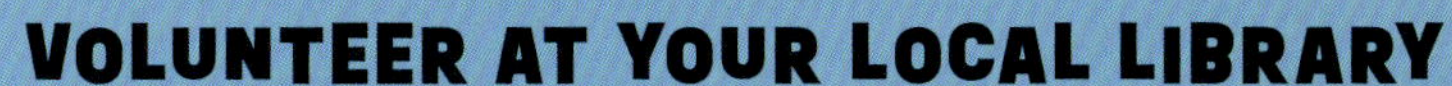

VOLUNTEER AT YOUR LOCAL LIBRARY

Spend some time volunteering at your local library. Caring for books in your community can help you feel proud and connected to the neighborhood you call home.

VISIT YOUR LOCAL FARMERS' MARKET

Grab some fresh fruit, vegetables, or handmade goods from your local farmers' market. It's a perfect way to shop locally and support small businesses.

TRY MAKING A PIECE OF JEWELRY

You can use braided yarn, beads, wire, and more to make fun and affordable jewelry at home. It's a great way to get creative and give yourself a small gift.

GO FOR A SLOW MORNING JOG

Starting your morning with a slow jog can help you stay active and clear your mind to prepare for your day ahead.

GIVE YOUR FACE AN ICE BATH

A quick ice bath for your face has benefits, like reducing inflammation or puffiness, easing the effects of acne, tightening your skin, and calming anxiety.

EAT A BOWL OF FRESH FRUIT

A bowl of fresh fruit is refreshing and good for your body. Cut up some of your favorites and chow down for a chill and healthy snack.

PAINT A CERAMIC MUG WITH A FUN DESIGN

Take some time painting a mug with a design that you would love to look at each morning.

GIVE YOURSELF MORE GRACE

It feels hard when we let others down or let ourselves down somehow, but allowing yourself a bit of grace can help you release guilt, learn, and move forward.

MAKE A BOWL OF STEAMING HOT CHILI OR SOUP

A delicious bowl of hearty chili or soup can warm you up from the inside out and does a great job of feeding your body.

GIVE YOURSELF A GENTLE NECK MASSAGE

Your neck can hold *so* much tension. Try a gentle neck massage throughout your day, and notice a difference in your posture and aches over time.

MAKE A COLLECTION OF HOMEMADE GREETING CARDS

Grab some card stock, gel pens, and markers to make your own collection of homemade gift cards. You'll have a great stash to pull from for the next wedding, birthday, or housewarming you attend.

BE MINDFUL OF TENSING UP YOUR BODY

It is easy to tense up as you move and interact with others throughout your day. Be mindful of relaxing your body to release tension as much as you can.

TRY YOUR HAND AT EMBROIDERING

Embroidery is as relaxing as sewing and crocheting. There are many embroidery kits available to help you learn how to master this textile skill.

BE FLEXIBLE WHEN IT COMES TO PLANS

Adulthood is nothing if not busy and ever-changing! Try to be understanding when your friends need to change plans, and offer yourself grace if you ever need to do the same.

TICKE
"Thanks for rescheduling!"
THE GUY

LEARN A NEW LINE DANCE OR ROUTINE

Line dances can be satisfying once you have all the steps down. Learn a new routine from the web so you won't ever be the only one standing still.

RESTART ONE OF YOUR FAVORITE TELEVISION SERIES

Restart your favorite comfort show and watch your favorite characters change or grow throughout the seasons.

HANG OUT WITH A FRIEND YOU HAVEN'T SEEN IN A WHILE

Life can get hectic, and catching up with a friend you haven't seen in a long time is a great way to cherish friendship and enjoy life.

TRY CALLIGRAPHY

The practice of calligraphy is super satisfying. Try focusing on the smooth strokes of ink as you go.

TAKE UP PHOTOGRAPHY

Capturing the places, people, and things around you can be a fascinating and relaxing hobby. Try your hand at digital and film cameras to find your favorite.

ENJOY A HOT SHOWER

Feeling clean after a hot shower helps you stay calm and content. Take some deep breaths and let your worries wash away.

WATCH A VIDEO OF
CUTE PUPPIES OR KITTENS
The cuteness overload of puppies and kittens
on the internet can be the perfect remedy
for a gloomy or overwhelming day.

PLAY A GAME OF I SPY

A simple game of I Spy is a great way to pay attention to your surroundings and be present where you are. Try to spy something cool!

TRY THE 5-4-3-2-1 METHOD

If you ever feel an anxiety attack coming on, reconnect with your mind and body by naming five things you can see, four things you can touch, three things you can hear, two things you can smell, and one thing you can taste.

SET A NEW GOAL

Challenging yourself is always a great way to experience growth. Set a new goal that is as big or small as you like and encourage yourself to make it.

REMIND YOURSELF THAT EVERYONE'S JOURNEY IS DIFFERENT

Your journey is yours for a reason. No matter your age or stage in life, know that your journey is as meaningful as that of the person next to you.

WRITE A LETTER TO YOURSELF TO OPEN ON YOUR NEXT BIRTHDAY

Take a moment to write about the moment of life you are in, with the intention of opening it on your next birthday—a chill way to enter a new age.

PRACTICE WEEKLY RESETS

Dedicate your Sundays to resetting your mind and space. You could do your laundry, complete a light clean of your space, and update your calendar for the week ahead.

FIND A PASSION PROJECT

Start a hobby or project that is strictly for your creative enjoyment. Prioritize pouring time into your project when you can.

TRY A PILATES CLASS

Pilates is a great way to move your body with intentional motions that are still challenging. Joining a Pilates class can help you feel balanced and in community with others.

REMEMBER, YOU CAN MEET NEW PEOPLE

It can be easy to shut yourself off, especially after feeling hurt or embarrassed, but allowing yourself to remain open to meeting new people and forming new connections is rewarding.

GIVE YOURSELF A TIGHT HUG

Wrap your arms around your shoulders and give a tight squeeze. This is a quick way to give yourself a jolt of self-love and regulate any overstimulated nerves.

DON'T BE AFRAID TO DANCE IN THE RAIN

Either literally or metaphorically, don't be afraid of a little rain. Allow yourself to dance when it begins to pour down in life.

HIKE TO A SCENIC VIEW AND ENJOY THE SIGHTS

Travel to a scenic park and enjoy the clarity and peace a nice hike in the woods can bring.

COUNT BACKWARD FROM ONE HUNDRED

A simple task you can do anywhere, out loud or in your head. Counting this way requires just a bit of focus and gives you time to breathe and reset your mind.

WATCH A THUNDERSTORM FROM YOUR WINDOW

Watch and listen to a thunderstorm from a window in your house. Be lulled by the downpour of rain, flashes of lightning, and roars of thunder.

DO ONE SMALL TASK YOU'VE BEEN PUTTING OFF

Procrastinating on small tasks is normal, but checking off that thing you've been meaning to do for months—that will probably only take you ten minutes—will be incredibly satisfying.

THINK ABOUT HOW FAR YOU'VE COME

When life feels chaotic or impossible, think about how far you have already come, and remember you can keep going.

SAY AN INTENTION EACH NIGHT BEFORE BED

Send yourself off to dreamland with intention. It can be how you will spend your day tomorrow or an intention to change something in your life.

LEARN TO TAKE CONSTRUCTIVE CRITICISM

Whether in a personal or professional setting, constructive criticism is a skill that will help you navigate through life. Try to see the help and support in the constructive criticism you may receive from others.

VALIDATE THE EMOTIONS OF OTHERS

Do your best to validate the feelings of the people in your life. Everyone wants to feel seen and heard every once in a while.

NOTICE SCENTS YOU ENJOY THROUGHOUT YOUR DAY

Be mindful of any delightful scents that you encounter and enjoy. Does a certain scent remind you of a happy memory or place?

LIMIT YOUR SOCIAL MEDIA TO THIRTY MINUTES A DAY

It can be easy to get wrapped up in your screen and ignore what's happening IRL. Try limiting your daily social media intake and the flood of images and information that can distract you from being present in other areas.

DON'T JUDGE YOUR FEELINGS

Rationalizing and judging your feelings isn't the same as actually *feeling* them. Give yourself time to feel and process your emotions without inner judgment.

TRY PLAYING CALMING SINGING BOWLS

Traditional Tibetan singing bowls provide beautiful sound frequencies that invite peace and deep relaxation.

APPRECIATE YOUR AUTHENTICITY

Taking a moment to appreciate the unique things that make up your personality and character can provide a strong sense of self identity and increase self-love.

MAKE A TIME CAPSULE

Spend some time collecting items that represent your day-to-day life. Bury it and plan to open it in five to ten years. This activity tends to build gratitude for the present and excitement for the future.

HAVE A READ-A-THON

Either solo or with friends, plan a read-a-thon: an entire day of reading and relaxation. Make it fun with your favorite snacks and a reading goal for the day.

REALIZE WHEN YOU ARE LOSING PATIENCE

Knowing your limits is a benefit for yourself and everyone around you. If you feel yourself losing patience, try to pause and regroup instead of pushing through any tasks or commitments with heightened frustration.

USE A TIMER OR ALARM THROUGHOUT YOUR DAY

Try using labeled alarms throughout your day to transition between tasks. This can help you stay productive and calm and remember important things on a busy day.

UNSUBSCRIBE FROM JUNK MAIL

Don't let junk clutter your virtual or physical mailboxes. Make space for the mail that matters to you.

REFLECT ON THE BEST MOMENT OF YOUR DAY

No matter how big or small, reflecting on the best moment of your day is a great way to stay mindful and grateful for the good.

REMEMBER, YOUR VOICE DESERVES TO BE HEARD

Try your best not to doubt your words and ideas. You have a voice that deserves to be heard like everyone else.

WRITE DOWN YOUR TOP PRIORITIES

Make a list of the top priorities in your life. This can help you feel organized and in control, in a chill way.

TRY TO APPRECIATE THE PRESENT MOMENT

Be mindful that the past is gone, the future is unknown, and all we have is now. Try to ground yourself in your present moment whenever you can.

TELL SOMEONE YOU LOVE THEM

We all need love. Be mindful of saying “I love you” to those you cherish—often.

TELL YOURSELF "THANK YOU"

Remember to tell yourself "thank you" for making it through each day and caring for your mind and body.

TAKE A POTTERY CLASS

Whether you've never done it or tried it one time back when, getting your hands messy with clay can feel exciting and rewarding.

TRY A PAINT-BY-NUMBERS BOOK

This is a calming activity that allows you to focus and be creative as a colorful image forms number by number.

PLAY A GAME OF SUDOKU

This ancient puzzle practice is a great way to kill time and relax. Try at different levels of easy, medium, or hard for a good brain scratcher.

TAKE THREE DEEP AND FILLING BREATHS

Three slow, deep breaths send a message to your brain that you are safe. This is a simple and effective way to calm your thinking or anxiety.

TRY TO DRAW YOUR FAVORITE ANIMATED CHARACTER

Think of your favorite animated character. Once you have a clear image of your character in mind or pulled up online, try to draw them in one sitting. No judgment!

MAKE A LIST OF MEAL IDEAS TO COOK AT HOME

Stay on top of eating delicious meals that are good for you by making a handy list of meal ideas that you can easily reference and make on the fly.

KEEP A JOURNAL OR NOTE CARDS OF FAMILY RECIPES

This archive of family recipes can help take away any anxiety of losing recipes when a family member passes on. Record the recipes that matter most to you and pass them along for years to come.

TRY PERFECTING A BAKED LASAGNA

Perfectly cooking layers of cheese, noodles, and your favorite fillings is a recipe for staying chill.

VOLUNTEER AT YOUR LOCAL PET SHELTER

Animals are among our most vulnerable, and caring for them in your spare time is a chill way to give back and get your fluffy fix.

TAKE A PICTURE OF YOURSELF ON EVERY BIRTHDAY

Try capturing yourself on each birthday to see how you change and grow. Soon you'll have a self-portrait archive to look back on as the years pass.

DRESS UP FOR A NORMAL DAY

Wear your fancy digs to add some simple joy to a normal day. You don't always have to wait for a special occasion to look nice on the outside and feel good on the inside.

TAKE A COOKING CLASS
Learning to make a new dish with the help of an instructor, and alongside new classmates, is one way to step out of your usual routine and do something exciting.

LIMIT YOUR PHONE NOTIFICATIONS

Take a breather and limit the notifications on your phone. Being constantly accessible by others can feel overwhelming.

TREAT YOURSELF TO A MANICURE AND/OR PEDICURE

A nice mani and/or pedi is a relaxing way to pamper yourself and stay chill. A set of smooth and well-manicured hands can also add to your confidence.

MAKE A MINDFUL BUCKET LIST

Think about the things you want to accomplish before you kick the bucket. Keep your list mindful by only adding experiences you truly care about or that bring you joy.

SEND OUT A SILLY HOLIDAY CARD

Take the stress out of sending out the *perfect* holiday card and just do something silly. Whether adding some silliness to your setting or making funny faces, your loved ones will appreciate a lighthearted holiday greeting.

VISIT YOUR CITY'S DOWNTOWN

There is so much to explore in every growing city. Try exploring the hustle and bustle of your city's downtown and see what your city has to offer.

VISIT A BEACH OR LAKE

Take a dip in a beautiful beach or lake. There are always moments of peace and chill waiting at the edge of water.

PLAN SEASONAL ACTIVITIES THROUGHOUT THE YEAR

Give yourself themed outings or events to look forward to throughout the year by planning seasonal activities. Bring on the pumpkin patches for fall or sunflower fields in spring.

ADMIT WHEN YOU ARE UNSURE OF SOMETHING

Honor yourself and your inner chill by admitting when you aren't so sure about something instead of saving face.

CELEBRATE FRIENDSHIP ANNIVERSARIES

Friendships are some of the most important relationships in life, and it's a wonderful thing to treat them as such by celebrating your friendiversary.

START OR JOIN A COMMUNITY GARDEN

Starting or joining a community garden is a great way to connect with those around you and beautify the place you call home. Plus, a healthy garden is great for the environment.

STOP AND SMELL FRESH FLOWERS WHENEVER YOU SEE THEM

This isn't a joy limited to fairy-tale princesses. Stopping to smell the flowers in life is a chill way to embrace the beauty around you.

FORGIVE YOURSELF AS MANY TIMES AS YOU NEED TO

Forgiving yourself releases so much built-up energy and regret that do nothing but hinder you. Forgive yourself as many times as you need to in order to feel peace and move forward.

ALLOW GRIEF TO COME AND GO

Grief is a lifelong journey, but allowing it to ebb and flow naturally is the only way to get through it.

TRY NOT TO OVERSCHEDULE YOURSELF

Be mindful of the amount of time you have in a day, and do your best not to schedule yourself so much that you run yourself right into the ground.

STRIVE FOR A BALANCE OF SOCIAL AND SOLITUDE

Socializing and solitude are both important areas of life. Finding a balance between the two will help you feel well-adjusted and connected with yourself and those around you.

FEED YOUR CREATIVE PASSIONS

Getting busy in life can often push creative passions to the wayside. Feeding your creativity helps you stay happy and allows your mind to wander blissfully.

DON'T DOWNPLAY YOUR SKILLS OR QUALIFICATIONS

There is a difference between bragging and being confident in your skills. Never downplay the skills or qualifications you have earned.

ALLOW PEOPLE TO CELEBRATE YOU

Remind yourself that you are worthy of being celebrated and receiving love from others.

SHOW GRATITUDE FOR DAILY LIFE

Try to show gratitude and thanks for the pleasures of your daily life that you may take for granted. This is a great way to remain chill and content with what you have.

PAY ATTENTION TO THOSE WHO SHOW UP FOR YOU, NOT THOSE WHO DON'T

While the absence of some people in your life may sting, do your best to cherish and focus on the people in your life who do show up and not dwell on those who don't.

NOTICE HOW YOU FEEL WHEN TAKING IN NEWS

Try being mindful of your nervous system when you are taking in news about the world. Staying informed is important, but don't allow yourself to be consumed by what you can't control.

PLAN A FUNNY PHOTOSHOOT WITH FAMILY

Try planning a funny photoshoot with family or friends to have a fun memory to look back on.

"Oui, oui."

TRY LEARNING A NEW LANGUAGE

Learning a new language can help improve your memory, diversify your résumé, and increase your ability to multitask.

PLACE A HAND ON YOUR HEART AND FEEL IT BEAT

Feel the rhythm of your own heart when you just need a reminder that you are here and doing your best. Cherish each moment you get to beat through.

LEAVE YOUR WORKDAY AT WORK

Try your best not to carry the weight and responsibilities of your workday home with you each day. A healthy work-life balance is key to staying chill.

IMAGINE A DIFFERENT ENDING TO ONE OF YOUR FAVORITE MOVIES

Let your fan-fiction mind run wild and reimagine the ending to one of your favorite, or least favorite, movies to make it better.

STAY CONNECTED WITH FRIENDS VIA POSTCARDS

Sending and receiving scenic postcards from a friend is a great way to stay connected, and you'll have a collection of postcards to keep.

REMIND YOURSELF YOU CAN DO HARD THINGS

You are stronger than you know and more capable than you can imagine. Remind yourself that you can do hard things without losing your head.

DO YOUR BEST TO SHOW UP FOR YOUR FRIENDS

Showing up for those you love is rewarding. Be sure to honor your own needs, but always do your best to show up for your friends and let them know you care.

SPRAY A CALMING MIST

A calming mist is a quick, refreshing spray that you can walk through and inhale to relax your senses. Find a mist with a scent you love, like lavender or eucalyptus.

EMPHASIZE A SENSE OF COMMUNITY IN YOUR LIFE

A strong community around you can offer perspective, comfort, and a lot of love. Do your best to form and sustain a community you care about.

TRY A HOBBY YOU LOVED AS A CHILD

You can dive back into something you loved to do as a child. Catering to your inner child can be healing and eye-opening.

TELL A FUNNY JOKE

Make yourself or someone else laugh with a quick, funny joke. You could try telling one a day and see how creative you can get.

VOLUNTEER WITH CHILDREN

Spend some time volunteering with children at your local community school or children's programs to help the next generation thrive.

PLAY WITH A JUMP ROPE

Jumping through the air over a rope to the rhythm of your choice is a simple pleasure that helps clear the mind while moving your body.

TAKE AN ICE BATH

Placing yourself in a tub of ice for at least thirty seconds can help decrease stress, soothe muscle aches, and stabilize your mood to ensure you are enjoying maximum chill mode.

HOLD AN ICE CUBE TO THE BACK OF YOUR NECK

Try rubbing a single ice cube up and down the center of the back of your neck. This is a nice shock to your nerves to feel more alert and aware without feeling overwhelmed.

SHAKE YOUR LIMBS FREELY

Shake away any stagnant energy by flinging your limbs wildly and freely for a set amount of time. Try starting with about twenty seconds and see how you feel.

HUG A TREE FOR A WHILE

Hugging a tree can help you feel connected to the earth around you and show gratitude for the nature you get to witness.

KEEP A PET ROCK

It may feel silly, but keeping a pet rock, or a collection of rocks, can help you keep your chill. Rocks can remind you to be resilient and not to shy away from stillness.

TEAR UP JUNK MAIL

Try ripping up the needless junk mail you receive and throwing it into your nearest recycling bin. This can help you release some frustrations and aid the environment.

STARE AT A LAVA LAMP

Allow your mind to take a break and wander as you watch the colors and textures of a lava lamp float in mesmerizing patterns.

READ A BOOK OF INTERESTING OR FUN FACTS

Feed your mind with a book of fun facts or brainteasers. Learning new things is super chill.

PRACTICE BALANCING SOMETHING ON YOUR HEAD

Balance is a great power and requires a lot of focus. See how long you can balance a safe object and connect your body and mind.

TIE-DYE A GROOVY SHIRT

The art of tie-dye did not die off in the '70s. Try hanging out and making different creations like a shirt, hoodie, or colorful tapestry to use as a handy picnic blanket or hang in your room.

LISTEN TO A NEW MUSIC ARTIST OR GENRE

Discover new music when you feel down. Hearing a new song or artist you connect with can help you awaken new interest and feelings of peace.

KEEP A SMALL ROSE QUARTZ STONE IN YOUR POCKET

Rose quartz is said to promote self-love and compassion. Carry a small stone of it with you as a reminder and an intention.

SAY THE ABCS BACKWARD

Try to say the ABCs backward if you find yourself needing a moment to breathe. By the time you make it from *Z* to *A*, your mind will feel calmer and at ease.

DO A FEW JUMPING JACKS

A set of ten to twenty jumping jacks, when you feel overwhelmed or anxious, can help you reset your energy and refocus your thoughts.

REARRANGE A BOOKSHELF BY COLOR OR ALPHABETICALLY

Take some time to appreciate your book collection by organizing the books in a satisfying manner.

CHEW A PIECE OF COOLING MINT GUM

Enjoy a cooling sensation and refreshing taste with a piece of mint gum—a small and easy way to add some chill into your day.

FOLD LAUNDRY VERY SLOWLY

Keep your chill by taking the rush and dread out of simple tasks, like folding a load of laundry. Try folding slowly and limiting yourself to one load at a time.

BELIEVE IT WILL ALL WORK OUT

Think about the situations in your life working out for the best before you think of them going wrong. Anticipating a good outcome can help you stay positive and make the best decisions.

REMIND YOURSELF BAD TIMES ARE TEMPORARY

Rough times are inevitable in life, but they don't last forever. Take comfort in knowing that the bad times you face will end, and you will be okay.

DONATE A FEW ITEMS YOU NO LONGER USE

Donating belongings that you no longer use is a more sustainable and giving option than throwing them away. Try dropping off a box or two of clothes or home goods you no longer have use for.

REARRANGE YOUR BEDROOM

Revamping your bedroom can welcome new energy and uplifting vibes into your space. Get creative about the small or big changes you want to make.

LISTEN TO A GUIDED MEDITATION

It can be difficult to clear your mind and focus when meditating on your own. A guided meditation is the perfect way to center yourself and reach the maximum benefits of meditation.

GO ON A WALK OR RUN AN ERRAND WITHOUT YOUR PHONE

Take some time existing in the world without your phone. Make sure you are in a safe and familiar environment, and enjoy your freedom from your cellular.

GO SEE LIVE MUSIC

Live music is an entirely different experience from streaming or listening to records. Feel the joy of seeing live musicians play at your local bar or music venue.

READ OR MEMORIZE A POEM

Witnessing the beauty of poetry and language is a great way to celebrate literature and stay chill.

SPEND TEN MINUTES PICKING UP TRASH IN YOUR COMMUNITY

Take some time to clean up the place you call home. Taking care of your community can help you feel settled and proud of where you live.

PRESS OR DRY PLANTS OR FLOWERS

Preserving flowers by pressing or hang drying is a fun activity that doubles as beautiful DIY decorations for your home.

LEARN HOW TO MEND YOUR CLOTHES

Learn how to sew or mend damaged clothing to help maintain a more sustainable and environmentally friendly closet.

BROWSE AT THE LOCAL LIBRARY

Find new reads and authors to add to your TBR list. Supporting your local library is the most chill you can get.

FORAGE FOR BERRIES OR MUSHROOMS

Try your hand at foraging berries and mushrooms to utilize in your meals. Be sure to follow expert advice to keep this activity fun and safe.

LEARN A MAGIC TRICK

Learn a chill magic trick that will leave your viewers scratching their heads and begging for your secrets.

JUMP INTO A BODY OF WATER

Diving into a body of water can be freeing and cleansing. Jump into your nearest safe body of water and set an intention before you rise to the surface.

RECORDS

MAKE A PLAYLIST OF YOUR FAVORITE SONGS

Curate a playlist just for relaxing. Queue it up whenever you need to unwind and hear what soothes you.

GO BROWSE A RECORD STORE

Browsing your local record store offers all the chill. Don't rush. Instead, ask questions, listen to music, and enjoy the vibes.

LISTEN TO JAZZ MUSIC

Soft jazz tunes can soothe your mind and help slow your heart rate. Let the music wash over you and carry away your worries.

MAKE A FLORAL ARRANGEMENT

Take some time to make a nice floral arrangement for yourself. Use a variety of flowers that will please your senses each time you walk by.

LEARN A SHORT DANCE CHOREOGRAPHY

Call a friend or turn on your favorite music video to learn some new dance moves. Don't judge your moves; just make them!

GO ON A COLOR WALK

Pick a color and try to spot objects of that color on a walk. You could even take photos each time you do this and make a collage from the collection of colors you capture.

LEARN THE NAMES OF THE PLANTS IN YOUR NEIGHBORHOOD

Try to get familiar enough with plant life to identify the trees and plants that grow in your neighborhood—a relaxing and informative activity.

HOST A SLEEPOVER

Host a good old-fashioned sleepover with snacks, movies, and friends to enjoy the nostalgia and make new memories.

CLIMB A TREE

Gain a bird's-eye view by *safely* climbing a tree. This is a childhood staple for most people that never loses its magic.

EAT AL FRESCO (OR GO ON A PICNIC)

Make a few of your favorite dishes and enjoy dining al fresco on a nice day. This is a great way to add some flare to a normal weekday meal.

TAKE A DANCE CLASS

Let the rhythm move you and enjoy learning with others at your skill level by joining a community of dancers.

MOISTURIZE YOUR BODY WITH AN AROMATHERAPY LOTION

Soft, silky skin is a great way to stay chill. Try an aromatherapy lotion that adds a relaxing scent to your moisturizing routine.

SING THROUGH A FAN

Also known as the original auto-tune, singing through a fan is a silly way to jam out to your favorite tunes.

TRY A RELAXING FACE MASK

Pamper yourself with a soothing avocado or charcoal face mask to soften both your skin and your mood.

MAKE A FORTUNE TELLER

Make a fortune teller with positive outcomes to mull over when you need encouragement or a reminder of your goals. All you need is a sheet of paper and a few markers.

MAKE A PUPPY PAW IMPRINT

A clay or stone imprint of your pet is a sweet gift to yourself or any other friend and dog lover you know.

EAT SOME FROZEN GRAPES

Enjoy the refreshing sensation of frozen grapes. Not quite hard and perfectly chilled, this is a delicious snack to munch on.

RUN AS FAST AS YOU CAN FOR THIRTY SECONDS

Sprint for thirty seconds to feel the exhilaration of your body in swift motion. Envision letting go of negativity and baggage along the way.

SCREAM INTO A PILLOW

Find a release by screaming out all of your frustration and pressure directly into a soft pillow.

TAKE A PERSONALITY TEST

Learn more about how you operate and what helps you succeed from trusted personality tests like Myers-Briggs or Enneagram. Knowing your personality is a great way to keep your chill.

COMMIT TO EIGHT HOURS OF SLEEP EACH NIGHT

Getting enough sleep sets you up for a productive and regulated day. Try to get in the habit of sleeping at least eight hours each night.

"Cool shoes."
COMPLIMENT SOMEONE
Paying someone a genuine compliment is a great way to spread kindness and make someone else feel special.

"Ditto!"

EXERCISE FOR TWENTY MINUTES A DAY

Moving your body for at least twenty minutes a day is said to improve overall health and happiness. Find what it is you like to do to stay active.

TRY READING YOUR HOROSCOPE

Check your horoscope for a little insight from the stars and moon; it's interesting hearing what they have to say about daily life.

DISCOVER YOUR LOVE LANGUAGE

From gift giving to quality time, learning your love language can be beneficial in showing yourself self-love and in your relationships with others.

TRY SOMETHING YOU'VE ALWAYS WANTED TO

Commit to doing something you've always wanted to but have often made an excuse not to try. This is your life, and there's always time to do the things you want!

RECITE YOUR FAVORITE SONG, BUT CHANGE THE GENRE

If you ever need a laugh or something to calm you down, try singing the words of your favorite song, but change the genre. Think "Don't Stop Believin'" sung as an opera.

ENVISION YOUR DREAM LIFE

Picture the life you've always wanted for yourself and never let go of that vision, even when things get tough.

SMILE AT YOURSELF IN THE MIRROR

The reflection of yourself you see each day can impact how you view yourself beyond the mirror. Try flashing yourself a smile after brushing your teeth or putting the finishing touches on your outfit.

PAINT A ROOM IN YOUR HOUSE A NEW COLOR

Try brightening up a particularly dreary room or area of your house with a new and bold coat of paint. This can liven up your space and the energy flowing through it.

SAY WHAT YOU NEED TO SAY

Silencing yourself is a recipe for feeling resentful and confined in your own expression. If something needs to be said, consider your delivery and say it.

WEAR A SUPER SOFT PAIR OF COZY SLIPPERS

Though not scientifically proven, it's nearly impossible to be upset while your feet are swaddled in cozy slippers. Slip into a pair after a shower and glide through your house.

MAKE A TIE BLANKET

All you need are two large pieces of cozy fabric and a pair of scissors to make this simple DIY blanket. Find a pattern that you love and make this your new favorite blanket to snuggle up with.

WORK SMARTER, NOT HARDER

Plan your workdays out and stay organized so you are able to get what you need done without being riddled with stress and deadlines.

YOU DID IT

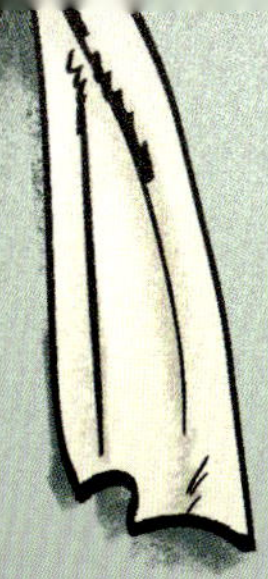

CELEBRATE YOUR WINS

Don't downplay your accomplishments—whether making it to work on time all week or completing a degree, you are worth celebrating!

GIVE YOURSELF AN EAR MASSAGE

An ear massage is very soothing and helps you focus. Begin at the bottoms of your earlobes and gently work your way up and down your ears for a few minutes.

REPEAT A DEEP "OM"

"Om" is a part of ancient Hindu tradition and is often used in meditation and yoga as a sonic release and acknowledgment of peace. Try saying a deep and filling "om" to reflect and center yourself.

CREATE A WORRY WINDOW FOR YOURSELF

If you need a moment, set a timer and allow yourself to worry and wallow as much as you need. Once that timer is up, try to move on with your day and not let your worry linger.

STOMP YOUR FEET

While throwing a fit as an adult is understandably frowned upon, stomping your feet around a bit is a great way to release tension and blow off some steam. To keep this tip chill for everyone, be sure to do this outside if you have downstairs neighbors.

POP SOME BUBBLE WRAP

Focusing on popping the small air bubbles can be satisfying and a great sensory experience. Relax and pop away.

BLOW RELAXING BUBBLES

Blowing iridescent bubbles has a special way of making you feel good. Picture your worries and troubles floating away in the bubbles and evaporating before your eyes.

BE MINDFUL OF CLENCHING YOUR JAW

Try to notice when you are going through your day with a clenched jaw. A lot of tension can be held in your face and jaw; remind yourself to relax multiple times a day.

LISTEN TO WHAT A CHILD HAS TO SAY

Children can often bring joy and even seem profound and enlightening without trying. Make children feel heard and confident in their voice at a young age.

SCREAM-SING

Find a neutral space where you can scream-sing to an irresistible ballad. Truly let loose and give it your all.

PRACTICE POSITIVE SELF-TALK

Make sure you are using positive self-talk, or internal dialogue, in reference to your appearance, accomplishments, and goals. Think of yourself how you would a good friend.

CHEW ON A PIECE OF DARK CHOCOLATE

Enjoy a bittersweet piece of dark chocolate, proven to be heart-healthy and good for brain function.

EAT A SOOTHING PEPPERMINT

A peppermint has a way of calming your nerves with its cooling sensations. Keep a few peppermints handy for moments you may need them.

RUIN YOUR ANXIETY

Imagine your anxiety is a flimsy piece of paper. Take a moment to crumple up that metaphorical piece of paper in your hands, hard, and throw it to the ground. You can even stomp on it for good measure. This is a reminder that you are in control, not your anxiety.

READ A COMIC BOOK

Read a popular comic book series and prepare to enter a visually pleasing, action-packed world. Comic books are entertainment, and collecting them makes for a cool potential hobby.

BUY YOURSELF OR SOMEONE ELSE FRESH FLOWERS

Make a habit of buying yourself or someone you care for fresh flowers to enjoy at least once a month. This is a thoughtful gesture that can show self-love and effort in relationships with others.

CELEBRATE YOUR JOURNEY INTO A CHILL LIFE

Allow yourself to learn and relearn all the ways to enjoy a chill life in an overwhelming world. Do your best and stay chill.

ACKNOWLEDGMENTS

Thanks to my family and my partner, Andy. Without you all, I couldn't have done it, let alone much else. A special shout-out to Insight Editions for being so patient with my nonsense.

ABOUT THE ARTIST

Phillip Bankss, or "philb," is a digital artist who posts his goofy scribbles to the World Wide Web. He lives in North Carolina with his partner. He one time drew a funny-looking dog a couple years ago, which led to YOU reading THIS.

weldon**owen**
an imprint of Insight Editions
P.O. Box 3088
San Rafael, CA 94912
www.weldonowen.com

CEO Raoul Goff
VP Publisher Roger Shaw
Executive Editor Edward Ash-Milby
Editor Kayla Belser
Managing Editor Michelle Hope
Art Director Megan Sinead Bingham
Production Design Jean Hwang
VP Manufacturing Alix Nicholaeff
Senior Production Manager Joshua Smith
Strategic Production Planner Lina s Palma-Temena

ISBN: 979-8-88674-394-4

Manufactured in China by Insight Editions

10 9 8 7 6 5 4 3 2 1